by Michael Scotto

cover art by Evette Gabriel

chapter art by Dion Williams

edited by Ashley Mortimer

typography by Kevin Dinello

Chief
For a
Day

By Michael Scotto

With Illustrations By
Evette Gabriel
& Dion Williams

LINCOLN
LEARNING
SOLUTIONS

Contents

CHAPTER 1

THE SUNNY DAY PICNIC

The last Thursday in July was a very special day in Midlandia. That was the day its citizens, the Midlandians, held their Sunny Day Picnic.

The Sunny Day Picnic was a festival to celebrate the season of summer. Every Midlandian got the day off from work. All afternoon, they flew kites, played games, held contests… and, of course, had picnics.

It was barely lunchtime, but the Midlandians had been preparing since dawn. All across Playland Park, they had set up tables, booths, and badminton nets.

Amidst all the hustling and bustling, a boy and a girl strolled together through the park. The boy carried a soccer ball in his arms. The girl had a picnic basket. They peered at the action all around them.

"Have you seen him yet, Violet?" asked the boy.

"Not yet, Zeke," replied the girl.

Zeke and Violet were searching for Chief Tatupu. He

was the leader of the Midlandians. Yesterday, Chief had given the pair orders to meet him at Playland Park today.

"I wonder what Chief has in mind for us," said Violet.

Chief had said that he had a very important job for the kids today. This was not unusual, though. Violet and Zeke were used to doing important things for the Midlandians.

Violet and Zeke were part of a special group of students known as the Kid Council. All through the year, members of the Kid Council took turns traveling to the island of Midlandia. While in Midlandia, they helped its citizens with their problems, both large and small.

"I bet he's still working at his office," said Zeke.

"I thought everyone had the day off," Violet replied.

Zeke shook his head. "I don't think Chief ever gets a day off," he said. "So, what now?"

Violet shrugged. Then, she lifted her picnic basket up near her face. "What do you think?" she asked the basket.

Zeke was puzzled. "Did you just talk to your lunch?" he asked.

Violet smiled. "This isn't my lunch, silly!" she replied. "I brought Belinda with me!"

Violet set down her picnic basket and opened its lid.

Inside was her pet kitty, Belinda.

"I have her in the basket to protect her from the sun," Violet explained. "I tried rubbing sunscreen on her once, but she hated it and her fur got all icky."

"Oh," said Zeke. "Does Belinda have any ideas, then?"

"Definitely," Violet replied with a nod. "She thinks that you should test me some more until Chief gets here."

"Works for me," said Zeke. "Let's get away from the crowd."

Zeke set down his soccer ball and dribbled it away.

"Hold on tight, Lindy!" Violet told her cat. She picked up the basket and hurried after Zeke.

Zeke and Violet found an open corner of the field.

"Ready?" asked Zeke.

Violet set down her picnic basket. "Give me your best shot!" she declared.

Violet was excited to play the game she had invented. Its rules were very simple. First, Zeke would tell Violet a month of the year. Then, Violet would name the federal holiday that happened during that month.

"May," said Zeke. He passed the soccer ball to Violet.

Violet stopped the ball with her sneaker. "Memorial Day!" she replied as she kicked the ball back. It skidded across the grass and stopped right at Zeke's feet.

"Nice kick!" said Zeke.

This might seem like a strange game, but at the moment, it was one of Violet's favorites. She was very interested in facts about the United States. Violet's family had moved there from China when she was only a few months old.

"Give me another one," said Violet.

"What happens during this month?" asked Zeke as he passed the ball.

"In July, we celebrate Independence Day," answered Violet. She launched the ball back to her friend.

Zeke juggled the ball between his feet. "What about November?" he called out.

"That's a tricky one," said Violet.

"It's easy!" cried Zeke. "In November, we celebrate Thanksgiving!"

"I know that," Violet replied. "But we also have Veterans' Day."

"Wait," said Zeke, puzzled. "You can have two federal holidays in one month?"

"There could be one for every day, I guess," said Violet.

"That would be neat," Zeke imagined.

"I don't know," Violet replied. "If every day was a

holiday, we'd never get any letters in the mail. And the garbage man would never come get our trash."

Zeke giggled. "That would *really* stink," he said.

Belinda meowed in agreement.

Just then, Violet spotted Chief Tatupu. He was walking near the gaming booths with a tall, thin Midlandian. She wore a shirt with a picture of the solar system on it.

"There he is," said Violet, pointing to Chief. "Who is Chief talking to?"

Zeke squinted in the bright sun. "That's Star!" he said. "She runs the planetarium. Let's go say hi!"

Zeke scooped up his ball. Violet hoisted her picnic basket. They both trotted toward Star and Chief.

From a distance, it had seemed like Chief and Star were having a conversation. But up close, Violet could hear that Star was doing almost all of the talking.

"No one in this town appreciates astronomy!" she was saying.

"Star seems upset," Violet told Zeke. "Let's wait until she's done."

The kids quietly followed Chief and Star.

"I have so much to teach, but no one will listen!" said Star.

Chief opened his mouth to cut in, but Star barreled

on. "There are orbits and axes, revolutions and rotations," she recited. "Stars and planets and comets and—"

Chief put a hand on Star's shoulder. "Hold on a moment," he was finally able to request. "I know that attendance at the planetarium has been down this year, but what do you want me to do about it?"

Star did not have a quick answer. "Well…" she began. "You could make a new law. Everyone would have to go to my planetarium once a week."

Chief chuckled. "Star, I do not think that is the fairest idea," he replied. "I can remind everyone about your wonderful planetarium. But if I forced every Midlandian to go, I would be giving you and your business special treatment. Plus, your guests would not enjoy their visit. It would be like doing a chore instead of having a fun evening out."

Star let out a dramatic sigh. "I clearly am not getting through to you," she said. "But no matter. I'm going to win Chief for a Day this year. And then I'll make the new rule myself! And that's a fact!"

Star stormed away. After a moment, Violet and Zeke walked up beside Chief.

Chief's mood brightened as soon as he saw the pair. "Oh, hello there, you two!" he said. "Did you happen to hear any of my conversation with Star?"

Violet and Zeke nodded shyly. "She seemed pretty upset," Zeke noted.

"I hate to disappoint my fellow Midlandians," said Chief. "But when you are a leader, you cannot please everyone."

"What did Star mean about making a new rule herself?" asked Violet. "And what's Chief for a Day?"

Chief knelt between the kids. "Chief for a Day is a very special contest," he said. "The winner gets to be Chief of Midlandia for one whole day—and I get to relax!"

"So you *do* get a day off!" said Zeke.

"Just one!" Chief replied.

"How do you pick the winner?" asked Violet.

"I will not be picking the winner," Chief said as he stood back up. "You two will!"

The kids were flabbergasted!

"Us?" asked Zeke. He and Violet had never even been part of the contest before, and now Chief had offered them the honor of being its judges!

"Most definitely," declared Chief.

"But… how does the contest work?" inquired Violet.

"Chief for a Day is one of Midlandia's oldest traditions," Chief explained. "It is a fishing competition."

Fishing was a popular pastime in Midlandia. It was Chief's favorite hobby.

"The Midlandian who catches the heaviest fish wins," Chief continued. "His or her prize is being chief tomorrow, from sunrise until sunset."

"So what do we have to do?" asked Violet.

"Your job has three parts," Chief replied. "First, you will announce the start of the contest. Second, you will judge which fish weighs the most. I have a special scale that you can use."

"A fish scale?" said Zeke, laughing.

Chief smiled and checked his pocket watch. "We should announce the start of the contest," he said. "Come, and I will explain the final part of your job."

CHAPTER 2

THE CONTEST BEGINS

Chief led Zeke and Violet toward a tall hill where several Midlandians were flying kites.

"Once you have chosen the heaviest fish, you can announce the winner of the contest," Chief instructed. "Tomorrow morning, we will have a special ceremony. There, you will hand the winner my crown and scepter. A scepter is a fancy wand. It is a symbol of being in charge."

"I want a scepter!" Violet exclaimed. "I'd use it to make my brothers change Belinda's kitty litter. Blech!"

Zeke was more interested in the crown. "You have a crown, like a king?" he asked.

"Indeed," said Chief. "I do not wear my crown often. It is a little too showy for me. But whoever wins the contest usually wears it the whole day."

"I didn't know that being a chief was like being a king," Zeke commented. "I thought it was like being a mayor, or maybe a governor."

"Being Chief for a Day can be whatever you want it to be," said Chief. "Usually, the winner will make up a new rule or holiday, or something like that."

"You must have a lot of weird holidays by now," Violet observed.

"Thankfully, any rules or holidays that the winner invents only last for one year," said Chief. "During the next Sunny Day Picnic, we will pick a new Chief for a Day and the whole thing starts over again! It is great fun."

The trio reached the hilltop, where they found a small, wooden stage. It had a microphone and a loudspeaker on it.

"Attention, Midlandians!" Chief said into the microphone.

The game playing stopped. Midlandians reeled in their kites. All eyes shifted to Chief and the kids.

"Welcome!" Chief called out. "Is everyone having fun?"

The crowd whistled and cheered.

"Belinda and I are!" Violet agreed.

"This is our best celebration yet," Chief announced. "From the North Pole to the South Pole, from the Eastern Hemisphere to the West, there is no place on the globe where I would rather be!

"But the best is about to come," he added. "We will now begin the Chief for a Day fishing derby!"

The crowd cheered even louder.

"Once the contest begins, you have until four-thirty to fish wherever you would like," said Chief. "Then, you must return to this stage with your catch. Violet and Zeke, would you two help me to kick things off?"

Chief lowered the microphone to the kids' height.

"Ready..." said Zeke.

"Set..." said Violet.

"Fish!" they shouted together.

In a flash, the crowd scattered.

Zeke turned to Chief. "What do we do now?" he asked.

"I am going to play at the skee-ball booth!" Chief responded. "With everyone gone, there will be no line at all."

"Can we go check out the fishing?" asked Violet.

"Of course!" said Chief.

Zeke chased his soccer ball down the hill. Violet trotted after him with her basket in hand.

For the rest of the afternoon, the kids walked from place to place. Anywhere there was a body of water, they found a fishing Midlandian. Each had a different reason why he or she wanted to win.

Wilda, the zookeeper, was camped out near a brook.

"If I win," she explained, "I'll make a new rule that everyone must take a little time to visit Animal Land. There is so much to see at my zoo!"

Cirrus, the meteorologist, fished on the muddy riverbank.

"When I become chief, I'll make a Weatherman Appreciation Day," he said. "I just hope it will be sunny out."

Builda, who made bicycles for a living, swished her fishing net through the pond near her factory. She was very proud of her pond with its fresh, clean water. She spent a little time there every single day.

"I don't have any special holidays in mind," she said. "I just want to make Midlandians happy. I'm a good boss at my factory. I think I'd do even better as chief."

Broadway, the actor and playwright, had a very odd way of fishing. The kids found him standing waist deep in Lake Midlandia. He was wrapped up from head to toe in white tape. He was wiggling back and forth in the water.

"What are you supposed to be?" asked Violet. "A mummy?"

"Gracious, no," Broadway scoffed. "That would be silly! Today, I am playing the part of a big, juicy worm! No fish can resist me. Oh, if I don't win the role of Chief for a Day, it will be a tragedy!"

The last Midlandian Violet and Zeke spotted was Star. They had been cutting through the forest back to Playland Park when they came upon her as she stood in the shadows. Star had cast her fishing line at the edge of a dark swamp.

"It's kind of creepy here," whispered Violet.

"And Star was in a bad mood before," Zeke remembered. "Let's just go."

But when Star turned toward the kids, she was all smiles.

"Oh, hi, kids!" she said. "Come on over. I won't bite! I just hope that a fish will."

Zeke picked up his soccer ball to keep it dry. He and Violet walked closer.

"I'm sorry you had to see my argument with Chief earlier," said Star. "I just get so worked up about astronomy! But that's no excuse for my behavior."

"Why do you love astro… astrono…?" Zeke struggled with the word.

"Astronomy?" replied Star. "I love it because it is jam-packed with fun facts. Astronomy even helped me pick my fishing spot."

"It did?" asked Violet.

"Astronomy is the study of outer space. That includes the moon," Star explained. "The moon looks different at different times of the month. Each change in the moon's appearance is called a moon phase."

"But what does that have to do with fishing?" inquired Zeke.

"Last night, there was a full moon over Midlandia," said Star. "It was very bright. On bright nights, fish come out to feed because it is easier for them to see the bugs that they eat. That makes them less hungry during the day, and, therefore, much harder to catch.

"Because I study astronomy," she continued, "I knew weeks ago that there would be a full moon. And I knew that every fish in Midlandia would be pigging out at the bug buffet."

"Ew!" said Violet.

"Every fish except…" said Star, raising her eyebrows.

"Every fish except the ones in this swamp!" Zeke exclaimed. "The trees here block out the moonlight, so the fish must be hungry here."

"That's a fact!" Star replied. Suddenly, her fishing

pole gave a jerk.

"Perfect timing!" she said. "This feels like a winner to me, kids. I'll meet you over at the weighing area in a minute. Chief for a Day, here I come!"

As Star reeled in her fish, Violet and Zeke hurried off.

When the kids reached the stage at Playland Park, Chief was waiting with his scale. A crowd of Midlandians had already lined up, each carrying fish in nets and coolers.

"Just in time!" said Chief. "Come on up!"

Broadway was at the front of the line. He was still peeling the white tape of his worm costume off of his clothes.

"Where's your fish?" asked Violet, noticing Broadway's empty hands. "Didn't you catch one?"

"Of course I did!" answered Broadway. "Well, I almost did. I almost caught a whole school of fish. I'll describe them for you! That's good enough, right?"

Chief grimaced a bit. "Sorry, Broadway," he said. "That would not be fair to those who actually caught fish. Better luck next year."

"Everyone's a critic!" Broadway cried. "It's a tragedy." He stomped down the hill.

"He will be okay," Chief promised. "Next, please!"

There were so many fish for Zeke and Violet to weigh! Or rather, there were so many fish for Zeke to weigh. Violet was mostly busy trying to keep Belinda from eating every fish.

"Lindy!" Violet hissed as she returned the kitten to her basket. "You are embarrassing me!"

"It's okay," said Zeke. He placed a fish on the scale. "She's probably just hungry."

Soon, Zeke had weighed almost every catch.

"Who's winning?" he asked Chief. Chief had been writing a list of all of the weights.

"So far," Chief quietly replied, "Star is in the lead. She caught a bass that weighed six pounds, five ounces."

Only Builda's fish had not yet been weighed. She stepped forward and heaved its heavy body on the scale.

"I think that'll… tip the scale in my favor," Builda said with a grin.

"Whoa, that fish is huge!" said Zeke. It weighed a whopping twenty-six pounds!

"We have a winner!" Violet announced.

"I knew it!" cried Builda. "I just knew my pond would come through for me."

Star frowned in disappointment, but she and the

other contestants clapped politely.

Zeke and Chief looked at the strange fish. It was bluish-gray in color. It had long whiskers around its mouth that looked like a mustache.

"What kind of fish is that?" asked Zeke.

"Gee," said Chief, scratching his bald head. "I do not recognize it."

"I know what it is," Builda said proudly. "It's a catfish!"

At that, Belinda burst from her basket. She leaped onto the scale and took a huge bite.

"Bad kitty!" cried Violet.

CHAPTER 3

CHIEF FOR A DAY

At sunrise the next day, Zeke and Violet returned for Builda's crowning ceremony. They met under a large tree in the center of the town square. It was known in Midlandia as the Great Tree.

"Where's Belinda?" asked Zeke. Violet usually brought her cat everywhere. But today, she was alone.

"Lindy wasn't feeling too well today," Violet replied. "She just wanted to stay in bed."

Violet held her hands behind her back. "I think I yelled at her too much yesterday," she admitted. "I feel really guilty."

"You're a lot more patient than I'd ever be," said Zeke. "That's why my poppa said I can't have a guinea pig."

Violet smiled. "I feel a little better," she said. "Thanks."

Zeke pointed to the community center across the road. That was where the Midlandians held most of their special events. It looked as if the whole town was filing inside.

"We'd better go," he suggested. "We have a crown to hand over!"

"And a scepter," added Violet.

Zeke and Violet entered the community center. They hurried to Chief's office in the back of the building.

"Welcome!" said Chief. "It is almost time for the ceremony."

Chief lifted two objects up from behind his desk.

"Wow," whispered Zeke.

The crown and scepter were made of solid gold. Each one was speckled with at least a dozen glittering jewels.

"Pretty fancy, eh?" Chief said with a chuckle. "Zeke, you carry the crown. Violet, you take the scepter."

The pair followed Chief to a large meeting room. Inside, every citizen of Midlandia was waiting in a chair.

Chief entered to loud applause. The kids followed with the crown and scepter.

Once inside, Chief began his speech. "We are gathered this morning to crown this year's Chief for a Day, Builda O. Bobo," he said.

Builda weaved through the rows of seats. When she joined Chief and the kids, Chief continued.

"With the help of our friends, I would like to present you with my crown and scepter," he said. "As you take them, you also take the title of chief."

Builda knelt in front of Zeke and Violet and closed her eyes. Violet handed her the scepter. Zeke placed the crown on her head.

"It's a perfect fit," said Builda.

"Now," Chief intoned, "rise, Chief Builda!"

Builda stood, and the audience stood with her to applaud. She bowed to the clapping crowd.

"Until sunset today, you have all of my privileges," Chief explained. "But you also have all of my chiefly duties, be they executive, legislative, or judicial. Be sure that you use your powers wisely."

"I will," Builda vowed, straightening her crown.

"Then I will join my fellow citizens," said Chief. He took a seat in the audience. Violet and Zeke stayed up front with Builda.

"I am so honored to be your Chief for a Day!" said Builda. "I don't have much time, so I have already prepared my first chiefly decree.

"Many of you wanted to win this honor," she went on. "In fact, I spent yesterday evening speaking with each of my fellow competitors. I was inspired by one Midlandian in particular. Star, please stand."

Star slowly rose from her chair. Zeke could tell from

her expression that she had not expected to be called upon.

"Star," Builda proclaimed, "in honor of your planetarium and all of your fascinating facts, I have decided to hold… a Solar System Celebration!"

Star looked like she was about to burst from happiness. Her eyes glittered like diamonds.

Builda waved her scepter over the crowd as if casting a spell. "At five o'clock, everyone will come to the planetarium," she ordered. "There, Star will enchant us with a tour of the sun, the planets, and their moons. I will see you there!"

With the ceremony over, the crowd began to scatter.

"You made Star's day!" Violet told Builda.

"Didn't I?" she replied, beaming.

"It was really nice of you, Builda," Zeke agreed.

Builda raised her eyebrow. "Excuse me?" she asked. She tapped her crown with a finger.

"Oh!" Zeke realized. "It was really nice of you, Chief Builda."

"Thank you!" said Builda. "Now, I am off to do my chiefly duties! Ta-ta!"

She marched off.

After Builda was gone, Zeke noticed that one Midlandian had stayed behind in his seat. It was Chief

Tatupu.

"What's your plan for today?" asked Zeke.

"Everyone else went fishing yesterday," said Chief. "Today, it is my turn. I am going to hunt for one of those strange catfish that Builda caught."

He pointed to the exit. "You two should help Builda," he advised. "She might not realize it, but being in charge is a lot of work."

"Sure thing, Chief!" said Violet.

"I am not chief today," he reminded the kids. "Today, you may call me by my real name: Manupu."

"Manupu?" asked Zeke with a smirk. "Your name is Manupu Tatupu?"

"Um..." Violet began. "Can we just call you Chief?"

Chief smiled. "Just do not let Builda hear you," he said with a wink.

Zeke and Violet followed Builda as she hunted for a problem to solve. Soon enough, she found one. It involved the twins, Fixit and Brushy.

Fixit was a doctor and Brushy was a dentist. They shared an office in the town square. Each day, they always made sure that at least one of them was in the office in case a patient came in.

"I want to go take my lunch break first," Fixit stated.

"But sis, I'm starving!" Brushy replied. "I missed breakfast. Listen to my belly. It sounds like there's a lion trapped inside."

"It's your own fault you skipped breakfast," she argued. "It's your turn to wait here."

At that point, Builda and the kids swooped into the room.

"I have a solution!" said Builda with a wave of her scepter.

"Chief Builda!" said Fixit.

"I heard your argument from outside," Builda explained. "Instead of taking turns to go out, why not have lunch delivered here? Then you can eat together!"

"That's a good idea," said Violet.

"Isn't it?" Builda replied. "Zeke, write down what these two want. You and Violet can fetch it from Bun's bakery."

That was how the whole day went. Builda would find a solution, and then she would send the kids on an errand to help.

Soon, it was five o'clock. The Solar System Celebration was about to begin.

"Wow, look at this place!" said Zeke.

He, Violet, and Builda had just entered the theater

inside the planetarium. Many Midlandians were milling about, chatting, and choosing seats. High above them all was a tall, curved ceiling.

Near the theater entrance, Builda and the kids were greeted by Chief Tatupu.

"Hey there!" said Violet. "Did you catch a catfish?"

"I was quite unlucky," Chief replied. "There were no fish biting at all! Perhaps I should have waded into the water instead of standing on the shore. How was your day, Chief Builda?"

"I was born to be chief!" Builda crowed. She shifted the crown on her head.

Chief smiled. "I heard that you have done well today," he said. "Sadly, the sun will set after Star's presentation."

"I have one more announcement to make after Star's show ends, if that's all right," said Builda.

"Certainly!" Chief replied.

Suddenly, the lights in the room began to dim.

"We should take our seats," Chief advised. He, Builda, Violet, and Zeke all sat together.

The room went pitch-black. After a moment, a bright, round, fiery image popped up in the center of the ceiling. The crowd began to "ooh" and "ahh."

"It's a picture of the sun!" whispered Zeke.

Then, Star's voice rang out in the theater. "Mercury!" she boomed. A picture of Mercury appeared. "Venus! Earth, our home. Mars! Jupiter! Saturn! Uranus! Neptune!"

One by one, each planet appeared on the ceiling.

A spotlight came up, revealing Star at the front of the audience. "So many planets with such strange names!" she said. "Even I have a hard time keeping track of them.

"I have a trick, though, to help me out," she continued. "I use a funny sentence that I made up. Each word in the sentence starts with the same letter as each planet. Would you like to learn it?"

"Yeah!" cheered the crowd.

"Here it is…" Star replied. "My very exhausted monkey just slept until noon!"

The audience laughed together.

"It looks like this show will be a hit," stated Chief.

It certainly was. For two hours, Star entertained everyone with stories about planets, comets, and groups of stars called constellations.

When the show ended, Star took a bow. Her guests gave her a standing ovation.

"Thanks, everyone!" said Star. "I'd now like to call up my friend, Chief Builda!"

Builda joined Star. "I have had such fun serving as Chief for a Day!" she said. "It is too bad that the day is about to end. There are so many more of you that I wanted to help."

The audience shouted in approval. Chief Tatupu whistled through his fingers.

"With that in mind," Builda announced, "I have created one final rule."

Zeke leaned toward Chief Tatupu. "What do you think it will be?" he asked.

"I bet that it will be something about keeping the environment clean," Chief whispered back. "Recycling and keeping the air and water clean are very important to Builda."

"The new rule is…" Builda said dramatically, "that I will stay chief!"

Some in the crowd clapped, but most Midlandians were just plain confused.

Zeke and Violet looked at Chief Tatupu. He was struck still with shock.

Builda raised her scepter. "Chief for a Day will no longer last from sunrise to sunset," she declared. "It will last through tomorrow! And the next day, and the next, and the next. I am your chief, and I am here to stay!"

CHAPTER 4

BUILDA'S RAINY REIGN

After Builda's startling announcement, Zeke and Violet had wanted to stay and help Chief Tatupu. Unfortunately, it had been time for them to go home for the weekend.

After what seemed like years, Monday finally came and Zeke and Violet returned. Zeke met Violet in the town square under the Great Tree.

"Check out all these clouds!" said Zeke. "It could rain any minute."

"Yeah," Violet replied in a low voice.

"You look as gloomy as the weather," Zeke remarked. He noticed that Violet had come alone again. "Are you and Belinda still fighting?"

"No, she isn't mad at me," said Violet. "It's even worse. She's sick!"

"Oh, no! I'm sorry," responded Zeke.

"My mom and dad took her to the vet for tests

yesterday," Violet revealed. "Lindy had to stay overnight. I'm so worried!"

"It's okay," said Zeke, patting Violet on the shoulder. "The doctor will give her medicine and take care of her. I'll bet Lindy will be good as new when she gets home."

"I hope so," said Violet. "My room was so lonely without her."

"I'll bet," agreed Zeke. "I feel like that about my house, sometimes, when my mom goes on trips for work. But you know what I do when I'm feeling down? I find something to keep me busy. When I'm busy, I worry less."

"That's a good plan," said Violet. "Let's focus on Midlandia for a while."

"Yeah!" Zeke replied. "We can go check on Chief."

They began to walk toward the community center.

"What do you think happened after we left?" asked Violet. "Builda made Chief pretty upset with her speech."

Zeke nodded in agreement. "I'll bet Chief told Builda that she couldn't change the rules," he said.

"And then he probably took that crown and scepter right back," said Violet.

"I wonder if Builda is in trouble," considered Zeke.

The kids passed by the wooden doors to the Portal Theater. That was where Broadway performed all of his plays.

Broadway was outside, holding one of the doors open. Brick, a construction worker, was carrying long pieces of lumber into the building on his shoulder.

"Start right there in the back, Brick," Broadway instructed.

The kids paused to greet their very dramatic friend. "Hey, Broadway, what's going on?" asked Violet.

Sounds of hammering began to ring out from inside the theater.

"The best of mornings to you, children!" said Broadway. "I've begun an exciting new project. I am adding some more rows of seats to my theater."

"Oh, cool!" said Violet. She always liked to attend shows at the Portal. She enjoyed concerts best. "Do you have a big, new show coming up?"

"Every show will be a big one from now on," Broadway replied. "Even these clouds cannot darken my spirits today. And I owe it all to Chief Builda!"

The kids glanced at each other.

"Wait," said Zeke. "Builda is still the chief?"

"Of course she is—and thank goodness!" said Broadway. "I'll admit, I thought it a little strange when she made her announcement on Friday. But this weekend, she made up Theater Thursdays. Now I'm a Builda believer!"

"What's a Theater Thursday?" asked Zeke.

"It's a glorious new rule that Builda made!" Broadway exclaimed. "Every Thursday night, all Midlandians will have to come see a show at the Portal. I'll never have trouble filling these seats again! Speaking of seats, I have to check on Brick in there. I'll probably see you Thursday!"

Broadway retreated into the Portal. The door closed behind him.

Zeke raised his eyebrows at Violet. "We really need to find Chief Tatupu now," he said.

"Let's check his office," Violet suggested.

The pair trotted into the community center. They made a beeline toward Chief's office.

But when they arrived at the open door, it was not Chief Tatupu behind the desk, but Chief Builda. She was in a meeting with Cirrus, the weatherman. Cirrus, wearing his raincoat, sat across from her.

"Let's wait out here," Zeke told Violet.

Inside, Cirrus sounded very upset. "But I don't make the weather," he insisted. "I only make predictions!"

"Then I think your title of weatherman is very misleading," Builda replied. "Perhaps you should be called the guesser-man. In fact, that sounds just right. I will make an announcement later today to tell everyone your new title."

Cirrus's chair scraped the ground as he bolted to his feet. "You can't do that!" he cried.

"Who is the chief of Midlandia?" asked Builda. "Is it you? Oh, I remember now. I am chief. And you are Cirrus, the guesser-man. Now, good day! Please close the door on your way out."

Cirrus sighed and exited the office.

Violet could see the sadness in Cirrus's face as he closed the door. "Are you okay?" she asked.

Cirrus turned, startled. "Oh, hello, Zeke and Violet," he said.

"What was that all about?" asked Zeke.

"Let's get away from here first," Cirrus replied.

He led the kids away from the office. Once they had turned a corner, Cirrus spoke.

"Did you notice the cumulus and stratus clouds in the sky today?" inquired Cirrus.

Violet shrugged. "We saw some kind of clouds," she replied.

"Those grey clouds mean that it will probably rain," Cirrus explained. "So, I predicted in today's forecast that it would rain, probably for the next few days. Of course, this was disappointing for some Midlandians. So Builda called me in and told me to change my weather prediction!"

"But that doesn't make sense," Zeke replied.

"Try telling that to Builda," said Cirrus. "I explained to her that rain is part of the water cycle. It just happens. But she wouldn't hear it. She even told me that I was showing poor citizenship because I predicted rain and bummed everybody out."

Cirrus and the kids reached the community center's exit. They opened the doors and saw misty rain falling from the sky.

"Good prediction, Cirrus!" said Violet.

Cirrus shook the right sleeve of his raincoat. A short umbrella dropped out of it into his hand.

"Do you kids have one of these?" he asked.

Violet and Zeke shook their heads.

"Then borrow my back-up," Cirrus replied. He jiggled his left sleeve and another umbrella dropped out.

"Thanks!" said Zeke.

"See?" Violet added. "Sharing an umbrella in the rain shows great citizenship."

Cirrus smiled. "By the way," he said, "what brought

you by that office?"

"We were looking for Chief Tatupu," Zeke replied.

"Do you know where he is?" asked Violet.

Cirrus thought for a moment. "I saw Chief early this morning as I returned a book at the library," he responded. "He and Dewey were looking through the *Rules of Midlandia*. That is a book that holds all of our laws and advice for their enforcement. They were trying to find a solution to this chief mess."

"I hope they find something soon!" said Zeke.

"Me too," Cirrus agreed. He lifted his umbrella and walked into the rain. "I don't think I can handle being called the guesser-man."

CHAPTER 5

THE CHIEF CHALLENGE

Zeke and Violet reached the Midlandia Library. Zeke shook the rainwater from the umbrella they had borrowed from Cirrus.

"Let's find Chief," Violet said.

The pair searched up and down each aisle. Finally, they glimpsed three Midlandians in the back corner of the library. They were seated around a table.

The first Midlandian they identified was Dewey, the town librarian. The kids could have spotted him from across town. Dewey always wore a red shirt with a big yellow "D" printed on it.

Next, Zeke and Violet recognized Sensei. He was a close friend and adviser to Chief Tatupu.

The kids almost did not recognize the third Midlandian. He appeared very tired and very troubled.

"Chief?" asked Violet.

Chief Tatupu glanced up at the kids. He looked as

though he had not slept all weekend. "Hello, friends," he said.

Zeke noticed a thick book open on the table. All three Midlandians had been studying it.

"Is that the *Rules of Midlandia* book?" he asked.

"You are correct," answered Sensei.

He and Dewey carried over two chairs from a nearby table. "Have a seat," Dewey offered.

Zeke and Violet sat at the table.

"Have you found anything that will help you yet?" asked Violet.

"Sadly, no," Chief replied. "We three have read every rule and law in this book. But we cannot find a single rule against what Builda did."

"Didn't Builda break the rules of Chief for a Day?" asked Zeke. "It's right in the name. She was only supposed to be chief for one day."

"That, my friends, is the trouble," said Sensei. "What Builda did was tricky, but it was not against the rules."

"But how can that be?" asked Violet.

"Any rules that the Chief for a Day creates must be followed as if they were made by Chief Tatupu himself," Sensei explained.

"Usually, the result has been something small," said

Chief. "A special holiday, for example, or a party."

"Like the Farmer's Ball the year that Harvest won," Dewey noted.

"Or," added Chief, "the contest winner might make a silly rule for the year."

"Like, everyone must eat more fruits and vegetables," said Dewey.

"Ah, yes," Sensei recalled with a chuckle. "When Doc Fixit won."

"Sheriff Badge drove herself bonkers trying to enforce that rule," said Chief, smiling a little. Then he sighed.

"But this year…" he trailed off.

"This year," Dewey jumped in, "Builda made it a rule that she gets to stay chief."

"I never thought that anyone would abuse the power of Chief for a Day," said Chief. "Midlandians just do not normally do such things. I guess I judged poorly."

Chief's sadness was making Violet feel upset, too. "But Builda doesn't deserve to be chief!" she argued. "She's just acting like a big bully."

"Now, now, Violet," Chief cautioned. "We should not resort to name calling. Yes, Builda is misguided. But her heart is in the right place. She wants to be chief so that she can bring happiness to all Midlandians."

"I don't know," said Zeke. "I think Builda is changing."

"How do you mean?" asked Chief.

The kids told Chief and the others about Builda's argument with Cirrus.

"That is most un-chiefly behavior," Sensei observed.

"She can't treat Midlandians like that," cried Violet. "Nobody even voted for her to be in charge."

Chief looked at Violet with a bit of embarrassment. "To be honest, Violet," he said, "no one ever voted for me, either."

Violet and Zeke looked at Chief in surprise. "Then…" Zeke began, "how did you become chief?"

"Remember how you said that being chief was like being a king?" asked Chief. "Well, in Midlandia, the role of chief is passed down from parent to child. That is another way being chief is like being king. My father was chief, my grandfather was chief, and so was my great-grandfather."

"That's different from America," said Violet. "America is a democracy. We have elections to pick our leaders, like the president. There are two main groups, the Democratic Party and the Republican Party. The person who gets elected is usually from one of those parties, but even that isn't a rule."

"You certainly know a lot about the government in America," remarked Sensei.

Violet flashed a beaming smile. "It's kind of my thing," she replied.

Zeke rested his head on the table. "It's too bad there's no way to vote for a chief," he said.

Suddenly, Dewey reached across the table and grabbed the *Rules of Midlandia*.

"Yikes!" said Chief.

Dewey flipped quickly through the pages of the book.

"What's up?" asked Violet.

"You kids just reminded me of something I saw in the book," said Dewey, scanning the text. "It's just a small section, way back… aha! The Chief Challenge!"

"The Chief Challenge?" asked Zeke. "What's that?"

"I'll read it to you all," said Dewey. He cleared his throat.

"'The most important quality in a chief is fairness,'" Dewey read. "'If a chief of Midlandia begins to punish or mistreat without cause, to give unequal favor to citizens, or to otherwise act unfairly, the problem may be solved with a Chief Challenge.'"

Dewey turned the page. "It goes on to say, 'In a Chief Challenge, one Midlandian citizen challenges the current chief to a vote for the title. The vote will happen exactly one week after the challenge. The whole population of Midlandia must vote. The winner with the most votes will be, from that day on, chief of Midlandia.'"

"That's an election!" cried Violet.

"I think you would win, Chief," added Zeke.

Chief thought for a moment. Then, he stood from his chair and declared, "A Chief Challenge it is!"

Violet and Zeke cheered while Sensei and Dewey clapped.

"We will round up some other Midlandians and bring them to the town square," said Sensei.

"There should be witnesses when you make your challenge," Dewey agreed.

"Very well," said Chief. "There is not a moment to lose. Come along, friends."

Zeke and Violet followed Chief out into the drizzling rain. The kids hurried along as Chief marched toward the community center.

Zeke was a very fast boy, but even he had trouble keeping up with Chief.

"Wow," said Zeke. "Chief means business!"

The three could soon see the community center. As they drew near, Builda knocked its doors open and exited.

She was wearing the crown and carrying the scepter.

Builda glanced back through the doors. Wilda the zookeeper followed behind her.

"I will test the pond water for pesticides," Wilda told Builda.

Builda smirked. "I've never used pesticides or other poisons," she said. "I only use non-toxic materials and renewable resources at my factory. And I would never pollute the pond."

"Whatever the problem is," said Wilda, "I will solve it."

"Your chief thanks you," Builda replied, making a small bow. "And remember, whatever you find, be sure to tell me first."

Wilda nodded and headed off toward Builda's bicycle factory.

"And I'll be sure to tell everyone about Wilda Wednesdays!" Builda called out. "From now on, every Wednesday will be party day at Animal Land!"

Chief and the kids finally approached.

"Excuse me," said Chief Tatupu.

Builda saw Chief and smiled. "Ah! Manupu Tatupu!" she said grandly, taking care to pronounce each syllable of Chief's name. "Or should I call you Manny?"

Chief ignored Builda's tone of voice. "Is there a problem at your factory?" he asked. He pointed toward Wilda, who was now just a small dot in the rainy distance.

"No, no," Builda stammered. "There is nothing for you to worry about… Manny."

She straightened the crown on her head. "Things are tip-top all over town," she noted, "now that I'm chief."

"Everything but the weather," said Zeke, wiping the rain from his face.

Builda squinted at Zeke. "Well, I'm working on that!" she snapped.

Zeke ducked back a little. He glanced behind Chief and Violet. Several Midlandians in rain slickers had begun to gather, led by Dewey and Sensei.

Violet raised her hand timidly. "Excuse me," she said. "Who is running your factory now that you're chief?"

Builda shrugged. "My workers all know their jobs quite well," she said. "The factory can run fine on its own."

Lightning flashed in the sky. Thunder followed a couple of seconds later.

"I had better get inside, Manny," she said. "I don't want my crown and scepter getting tarnished. Toodle-oo!"

"It is too late for that, Builda," said Chief. "You have

been acting unfairly since you became chief. You have given special favors to some Midlandians. You have treated others most unkindly. With that behavior, you have already tarnished the crown."

"I have no time to be lectured, Manupu Tatupu," Builda retorted.

"Then make time for this!" Chief announced. "I issue to you… a Chief Challenge!"

CHAPTER 6

HOLIDAYS OF THE WEEK

The news of the Chief Challenge spread faster than a brush fire. By the first night, everyone in town had heard. By the next, Midlandians had started to choose sides.

Zeke and Violet worked hard all week to help Chief Tatupu. They told everyone about Chief's honesty and fairness.

Meanwhile, Builda worked to win votes for herself. She shook hands with Midlandians at the zoo during Wilda Wednesday. She gave a speech at the Portal Theater during Theater Thursday.

Builda even created a new rule. She called it Muffin Mondays. Every Monday morning, each Midlandian would have to go to Bun's bakery and buy a snack.

To thank Builda, Bun put a special note inside each of his tasty treats. The note read: "Be a Builda Believer!"

Soon, it was Saturday. Usually, the kids stayed at home with their families on weekends. But the vote for chief was only two days away, so Zeke and Violet made an exception.

The sun was back out. Zeke bounced his soccer ball under the shady Great Tree. Violet bounded toward him carrying a backpack.

"You're in a good mood today," Zeke commented.

"I sure am!" replied Violet. "I have great news!"

"Did you get more Midlandians to vote for Chief?" asked Zeke.

"It's not about that," Violet told him. "It's about Belinda!"

Zeke stopped bouncing his soccer ball. He had not heard about Violet's kitty almost all week. Since Belinda had gotten sick, Violet had not wanted to talk about her much.

"We saw the vet again yesterday," Violet explained. "He said that Belinda was very sick, but she's going to be fine!"

"That's great!" cried Zeke. "Did the doctor figure out what was wrong?"

"He did," said Violet, "but it was all pretty complicated. The disease was called ent… enter… it had a weird name. It was hurting the organs in one of her body systems, the digestive system."

Zeke knew that the digestive system handled food and drinks. "So she got sick from something she ate?" he asked.

Violet nodded strongly. "I think it was that catfish she nibbled on," she said. "The vet told us to be extra careful about what Belinda eats from now on. I have to make sure she gets plenty of exercise. That will help her body to be really strong."

Zeke smiled. "I'm glad that Belinda will be okay," he said. "I hope she's strong enough to come back soon."

"Me too," said Violet. "But let's get to work for now. I brought some supplies." She patted her backpack.

"What's in there?" asked Zeke.

Violet unzipped her backpack. She pulled out a stack of flyers and a roll of tape. "Builda has that saying, 'Be a Builda Believer,'" she said. "I was so happy last night that I made up a saying for Chief!" She showed Zeke the stack. On each sheet of paper, Violet had neatly printed "Trust in Tatupu!"

"Hey, that's catchy," said Zeke.

"It was either this or 'Tatupu Is the One for You-pu,'" said Violet.

"I think you picked the better one," said Zeke with a giggle. "Let's go tape these flyers up."

The pair toured the town square. They taped a poster to every lamp post, tree, and bench. Eventually, though, Zeke and Violet reached a building that already had posters on it.

The posters were colorfully painted. Builda's saying, "Be a Builda Believer," was written on them in fancy, cursive lettering. They also had an image of Builda on them, wearing her crown and smiling.

"These are a lot nicer than my posters," said Violet, smirking.

"Of course they are," said Zeke. He pointed to the sign above the building's door. "Look whose place this is!"

The kids were standing outside the art gallery and studio of Midlandia's most famous artist, Vincent Van Wannadogood.

"Do you hear something?" asked Violet. She and Zeke leaned closer to the door.

Zeke heard a clinking sound inside. "Let's check it out," he said.

The kids entered Vincent's gallery. The clinking got louder. But the gallery seemed empty except for the many paintings on the walls.

"It's coming from in back," said Zeke.

The kids walked to the back of the gallery. When they rounded the corner, they saw Vincent in his studio. He stood on a step ladder in front of a very tall piece of marble. He had a hammer and a chisel in his hand. He was using them to chip away at the marble. Every time he hit the chisel, it made a loud *clink*.

"Vincent?" said Violet.

Vincent turned, still chipping away. "Salutations, my young pals!" he shouted over the clinking.

"What are you working on?" asked Zeke.

"I am making a monument for Chief Builda!" he exclaimed.

Vincent leaned aside. The kids could see part of Builda's face carved out of the marble.

"It looks like she's trapped in there," Zeke said quietly. "Hello, nightmares."

"It'll look much better when I'm finished," Vincent assured the kids. "When I'm through, this piece of art will go right next to the Great Tree! It will be like two landmarks in one."

Vincent glanced at his work. "Chief Builda wanted it in time for the vote on Muffin Monday," he said. "But this kind of work takes a really long time. Especially when my nights are so full at the zoo, the theater… I just hope that Builda doesn't take away my Sculpture Sundays!"

"Sculpture Sundays?" asked Violet. She hadn't heard about those.

Vincent flashed a pearly smile. "After Chief Builda asked me to make this monument," he said, "she offered me my very own day of the week! On Sunday nights, everyone has to come to my gallery!"

"Builda's going to run out of days to give away soon!" said Zeke. "There's Monday, Wednesday, Thursday, Sunday..."

"And don't forget about Solar Saturdays!" stated Vincent. He instantly stopped chipping.

"Oh, no!" said Vincent. "I won't be able to work tonight, either! I have to go to the planetarium for Solar Saturday. Chief Builda decided to make Star's celebration a weekly event."

Zeke and Violet looked at one another in disbelief.

Vincent began chipping as quickly as he could. He glanced away from his work toward the kids. "I'm sorry, you two," he said, "but I'm in quite a—yeeowch!"

Vincent's chisel slipped and he hammered himself right on the thumb!

"Ow, ow, blast it..." Vincent moaned, bounding down from his step ladder.

"Are you okay?" asked Violet, her voice full of worry.

Vincent was bent over, breathing deeply. "No worries," he whimpered. "I'll be fine!" He tried to give the kids a thumbs-up, but he cried out in pain.

"You're definitely not fine," said Zeke. He tucked his soccer ball under his arm. "We're going to Doc Fixit's office."

The kids helped Vincent across the town square. They quickly reached the office that Doc Fixit shared with her dentist brother, Dr. Brushy.

Violet opened the office door for Vincent. Inside, she saw Doc's desk and her posters of skeletons, organs, and the food groups. But Doc herself was nowhere to be found.

"Doc?" Zeke called out.

"She's gone," a voice said. It was Brushy. He was seated by the window on his half of the office.

"Did Doc go to lunch?" asked Violet.

"No," sighed Brushy. "She moved her office. I'm all alone here now."

Zeke's eyes went wide. "Did you have another fight?" he asked.

Brushy shook his head. "It was Chief Builda's idea," he said. "There was an accident at the bicycle factory last night. One of the workers hurt his leg. Chief Builda had Fixit move her office to the factory to keep an eye on things there."

"Let's hurry over," said Vincent, wincing. "I should be working!"

"One last thing," said Violet. She handed Brushy one of her flyers.

Brushy read the flyer's words: "Trust in Tatupu."

"You don't have to tell me twice," pledged Brushy. "I'd give anything to have things back to normal. I miss having my sister around. I don't think I can wait a whole week to visit her."

"What's in a week?" asked Violet.

"Why," Brushy replied, "Fixit Friday, of course."

CHAPTER 7

POND PROBLEMS

Zeke and Violet led Vincent into Doc Fixit's new office. It was in the basement of Builda's factory.

"Plaster of Paris!" cried Doc Fixit. "Your thumb is purple."

"It's no big deal," Vincent replied, though he was in much pain. "It's a very pretty color. It might inspire my next painting!"

"Don't listen to him," Zeke warned. "He's just worried about finishing his new sculpture."

Doc smiled. "I'll take good care of him," she promised. She sat Vincent in a chair. She carefully took Vincent's hand to give it a closer look. "Oh, my," she said. "I think you should skip the sculpting for a few days."

Vincent shrieked in horror. Then, he passed out in his chair.

"What happened now?" asked Zeke, running over.

"He just fainted," said Doc. "He certainly is nervous

about that project!"

"It's for Builda," stated Violet.

"Aha," said Doc, nodding thoughtfully. "That explains things. Well, you two can run along now. Maybe I'll see you tonight at the Solar Saturday party."

Just before she and Zeke left, Violet remembered something Brushy had said. "By the way, Doc," she said, "Brushy really misses you."

Doc fetched an ice pack and a pillow for Vincent. "I miss him, too," she said. "Can I tell you a secret?"

"You can always trust the Kid Council," Zeke replied.

"I really don't like being here," whispered Doc.

Violet looked around the dark and dank room. "I wouldn't either," she said. "Basements are scary."

Doc shook her head. "I mean being at the factory at all," she said. "I'm far from my brother and that's bad enough, but this place seems very different, too."

"What do you mean?" asked Violet.

"I mean," Doc replied, "that when Builda was running the factory, it looked like the best place to have a job! Every employee was in a good mood. They were proud of their work.

"But without Builda running things... no one here seems to be very happy," Doc continued. "They feel like

Builda doesn't care about them. So they don't care as much about their work, either. I think that's why there have been more accidents since Builda left."

Doc sighed. "This is a very different place," she said. "But I guess Builda's pretty different now, too."

The kids exited the bicycle factory. Outside, Zeke set his soccer ball on the ground. He tried to pass it to Violet, but it went right by her. The ball rolled downhill and splashed into the pond outside the factory.

"Aw, man," Zeke complained. "Hey, Violet, are you there?"

Violet turned to him. "Why do you think Builda changed when she became chief?" she asked.

Zeke shrugged. "I'm not sure," he said. He pointed to the pond. "When we first saw her over there, she wanted to be chief to do things that would make the Midlandians happy. But she's been going about it all wrong and is being very unfair."

"I think it's really hard to be fair and make everybody happy at the same time," Violet said. "My brothers get into fights about that kind of stuff. Something my one brother wants might make another one angry or get in his way."

Violet noticed Zeke's ball in the pond. It had floated

a few feet across the water. "Sorry about that," she said. "I was distracted, I guess. Let me go get it for you."

"Thanks," Zeke replied.

The kids walked over to the pond. Violet removed her shoes to wade into the water.

Just before she stepped in, though, a voice shouted to her, "No! Wait!"

"Stay out of the water!" another voice yelled.

Zeke and Violet whipped around. They saw Wilda and Beaker, a scientist from the University of Midlandia. Wilda had a large bag in her hands. Beaker had a magnifying glass and a test tube. The two Midlandians were sprinting toward the pond.

"Did you touch the water?" Wilda demanded.

Violet was very startled. "No, I didn't," she said.

Beaker sighed in relief. "That was close," she said.

"What's wrong with the water?" asked Zeke. "I just want my ball."

Wilda and Beaker glanced at each other. "I guess we have to tell them," said Wilda.

"Tell us what?" wondered Violet.

Beaker pointed to the pond. "This whole pond, and every fish in it, is very contaminated," she said.

"Contaminated?" asked Zeke.

"Filled to the gills with germs," Wilda explained.

"The germs are too small to see with your eyes," added Beaker. "But under a microscope, they appear huge. And boy, do they look nasty!"

Zeke and Violet took a swift step back from the shore. Violet yanked her shoes on.

"As long as you don't touch the water, you should be fine," said Wilda. "I wish I could say the same for the fish in there. The fish are very sick."

"Oh, no!" said Violet. "How can you help make the fish well again?"

Beaker looked at her grimly. "There is no drug or vaccine we can give them," she said. "We just have to wait for the germs to pass. It could take weeks. Some of the fish might not get better at all."

Wilda opened her bag and pulled out a net, a bunch of wooden sticks, and a long roll of yellow tape. The tape had "Keep Out" printed on it, over and over.

"I have these sticks and tape to put around the whole pond," she said. "We can put the sticks in the ground. They will hold up the tape."

Violet was thinking about her kitty, Belinda, and her illness. "Could the germs in the water have come from a catfish?" she asked.

"Yes, they could have!" said Wilda.

"We have a theory about it," Beaker declared.

"She means," stated Wilda, "we have an idea about how this whole mess might have happened."

As the team of four put up the tape, Wilda and Beaker took turns explaining their theory.

When the Midlandians finished, Zeke and Violet were stunned.

"Chief Tatupu needs to hear about this," said Violet.

Wilda and Beaker looked at her nervously. "We've been afraid of getting Builda in trouble," said Beaker. "I mean, she even gave Wilda her own special day of the week!"

"But the kids are right," Wilda agreed. "The time has come."

Wilda fished Zeke's ball from the pond with her net. She washed it with rubbing alcohol before she gave it back. Once the ball was clean, the foursome searched for Chief Tatupu.

They found Chief at Playland Park. He was speaking with a Midlandian named Knute O. Bobo. His nickname was Coach, because he ran all of the games at Playland.

"I cannot promise you any special holidays or favors," Chief told Coach. "But I do promise to treat you—and every other Midlandian—fairly and equally."

Coach shook Chief's hand. "You've got yourself an alliance!" he said. "Consider me to be on Team Tatupu."

Coach trotted off toward the kickball field.

Chief turned and faced the kids, Beaker, and Wilda. "Hello there!" he said. He noticed the anxious looks on Beaker and Wilda's faces. "Is something the matter?"

"We'd better start at the beginning," said Wilda.

CHAPTER 8

THE CATFISH CONFRONTATION

Zeke, Violet, Chief, Wilda, and Beaker found a set of bleachers and sat together. Wilda began to tell her story.

"On Monday," she said, "Chief Builda called me into her office. She was worried. There was a problem at the pond near her factory. She said the fish were acting weird. She told me that she would make a special holiday, Wilda Wednesday, if I could help and keep quiet."

"I remember hearing a little bit of your talk," Chief noted.

"When I saw the fish," Wilda continued, "they were all covered in weird spots. They were swimming slowly and did not seem hungry. I knew they were sick, but I didn't know why or how it had happened. So I asked Beaker for an extra hand."

Beaker took over. "We worked together all week. We took samples of the fish and the water," she said. "Using my microscopes and other technology in my lab, we found germs. Lots of them! I had never seen such germs. I had to look them up at the library."

"Here's the thing about germs," said Wilda. "Different germs affect different animals. Some animals can carry a germ around and it won't bother them. But that same germ can make other kinds of animals very sick. That is one reason we keep certain animals apart at the zoo."

"The germ we found," Beaker explained, "is common among catfish. It does not make them sick. But it makes many other kinds of fish sick."

Wilda added, "And also humans, Midlandians—"

"And kitty cats," Violet chimed in.

"You are just lucky that you did not catch any fish at the pond," Zeke told Chief.

"That is lucky," said Chief. "If I had had my way, I would have been eating catfish for dinner Monday night."

"And you could have ended up as sick as my Lindy!" cried Violet.

Wilda raised her pointer finger. "Actually, that leads into the next part of my story," she said.

"Builda caught a catfish at her pond," Wilda began. "I thought that was odd, even the day of the competition. Catfish don't usually live in Midlandian waters. I had never seen one outside of Animal Land."

"I think I said the same thing that day," Chief remarked.

"It gets even stranger," said Violet.

Beaker jumped in with excitement. "Once we learned about the catfish germs, Wilda and I went back to the pond. We wanted to catch another catfish for testing," she said.

"We searched the whole pond," Wilda stated. "We used nets, fishing rods, juicy worms...."

"We even used a special fishing invention that I had made," said Beaker. "It is a lure that sends out waves of communication to get a fish's attention. It's quite a dazzling creation. The way it works is—"

"Beaker..." Wilda warned. Beaker often got carried away talking about her inventions.

"Yes, right," said Beaker. "Anyway, we had no better luck than you did, Chief."

"Except that... maybe luck had nothing to do with it!" said Zeke.

Chief raised his eyebrows. "What do you mean?" he asked.

Wilda took a deep breath. "We think that there's a reason Builda caught a catfish and no one else did," she said.

"Builda put that catfish in her pond," said Violet. "That way, she could be sure to catch the biggest fish and win Chief for a Day."

Chief quietly looked at the others. "That is a very serious accusation," he said.

"It would explain why the pond and the fish got contaminated so suddenly," argued Beaker.

"And it would explain why Builda wanted me to keep quiet about anything I found at the pond," claimed Wilda.

Chief stood from the bleachers. "There is only one way to handle this," he said. "I will speak with Builda."

For the second time in a week, Zeke and Violet followed Chief to the community center. Beaker and Wilda stayed behind. They were afraid of how Builda would react to Chief's questions.

"What are you going to say to Builda?" asked Zeke.

"I will be honest," Chief replied. "I am not sure yet."

Chief led the way into the community center. He knocked on the door to his old office.

"You may enter!" Builda called from inside.

Chief opened the door. Inside, Builda was seated at the desk. The scepter was on the desk in front of her and she was wearing the crown. She was also wearing something new.

"Kids! Manupu!" said Builda. "How do you like my new cloak?" She stood up and let the long cloak fall around her.

Even though Violet was rather mad at Builda, she could not tell a lie. "It's beautiful," said Violet.

Beautiful was barely strong enough a description. The cloak was made from the finest material. All across it, bright gold and red threads were sewn into a very detailed pattern.

"Sew the seamstress made it for me," said Builda. "Well, she did the stitching, anyhow. I thought up the pattern. I guided her through the design process myself."

Chief was silent and very still. Zeke looked at him nervously. He knew that Chief only got this way when he was very upset.

Builda took no notice. "This crown and scepter are nice," she stated. "But I think that this cloak truly says 'Chief!' It will be perfect to wear after I win this silly challenge of yours."

Finally, Chief stepped up to the desk. "We have to talk," he told Builda.

"Oh, have you come to withdraw your Chief Challenge?" inquired Builda.

Chief Tatupu looked Builda in the eye. "Where did

that catfish you caught come from?" he asked.

Builda glanced away. "I caught it in my pond," she replied. "Remember?"

"I mean," Chief pressed on, "how did it end up in your pond to begin with?"

Builda hesitated. "How should I know?" she shrugged. "I'm no fish expert."

"Maybe not," Chief replied. "But surely you remember where you bought it."

Builda squinted at Chief. "What are you trying to say?" she asked.

"Catfish do not live in Midlandia," said Chief. "It is not their natural habitat. The fish you caught had to have come from somewhere else. I think that you brought the fish here and put it in your pond."

"That way," said Zeke, "you would catch the biggest fish and become chief for sure."

"And that's why the pond is all messed up," added Violet.

Builda's face scrunched into a scowl. "You've been talking to Wilda, haven't you?" she growled. "That little blabbermouth!"

"Do not get upset with Wilda," said Chief. "She is not the one who tried to cheat at Chief for a Day."

"I did not cheat!" Builda bellowed. "I just knew that I would be a better chief than anyone else. I knew that for certain, so I had to make sure the crown went to the right Midlandian.

"Maybe I did order in a special fish to catch," she said with a sneer. "But there's no rule against that. I still won the fishing derby, fair and square."

"True, there is no rule against what you did," Chief agreed. "However, that does not mean that you won 'fair and square.' How do you think the other contestants would feel if they learned the truth?"

Builda was silent. She knew just how the others would react.

"Was winning so important?" asked Chief. "So important that you were willing to pollute your own pond?"

Builda looked at him in shock. "Pollute?" she sputtered. "I have the cleanest water around! You know that. I'd never pollute it. All I did was add one fish."

Chief told Builda what he had learned about catfish germs from Wilda and Beaker.

"The fish in the pond are very sick now," said Violet.

"Some of them might not even survive," Zeke noted.

"And it could be months before the germs clear away,"

Chief finished.

Builda looked at Chief with red eyes. She was no longer angry. She only seemed sad and worried.

"What are you going to do?" she asked Chief Tatupu.

"Me?" he replied. "I am not going to do anything."

The kids looked at Chief in surprise.

"If I told everyone just what you did, they might never forgive you," said Chief. "It will do much more harm than good."

Builda breathed a sigh of relief.

"But you know how you won," said Chief. "And you know what the consequences have been."

He and the kids headed for the door.

"What happens next is all up to you," Chief told Builda. "That is why you wanted that crown in the first place, right?"

CHAPTER 9

VOTING DAY

Builda was quiet for the rest of the weekend. Solar Saturday came and went. Builda made no new announcements or speeches. She did not even come to Sculpture Sunday to see Vincent's unfinished monument.

Soon, it was Monday morning—the day of the Chief Challenge. Zeke and Violet met at their usual spot under the Great Tree.

"Hey there, Violet," said Zeke with a wave.

"Where's your soccer ball?" asked Violet.

"Oh, I left it at home," Zeke replied. Even though Wilda had cleaned the dirty pond water off of it, he had not much felt like carrying the ball around since.

"Then you can help me lug this around!" said Violet. She held out a picnic basket.

"Is that who I think it is?" asked Zeke.

Violet nodded happily. "Say hi, Lindy!" she said into the basket.

The top of the basket popped open and Belinda the cat lifted her head into the sunlight. She greeted Zeke with a quiet meow. Zeke even thought he saw her wave with her little paw. But Belinda ducked back under cover before he could be sure.

"She's much better now," said Violet. "So where are we supposed to go for the vote?"

Zeke pointed across the town square toward the Portal Theater. The Portal had a fancy curtain over its wooden doors. "The vote happens on the stage in a little while," he said. "But first, we have to go buy a muffin. It's the law."

"Oh, yeah, I forgot about Muffin Monday," Violet replied.

The kids hiked down the street to Bun's Blueberry Bakery and Bistro.

"Look at this line," said Zeke. "It's so weird!"

There was a long line outside Bun's, but that was normal for any morning. What Zeke found strange was the attitude of everyone in line.

The kids had never seen a group of Bun's customers look so unhappy to be there.

Zeke saw Posta, who delivered the mail in Midlandia, at the back of the line. He and Violet hopped in behind her.

"What's wrong with everyone?" asked Violet.

Posta looked back. "This is so silly," she said. "I'm supposed to be out working! How am I supposed to get all of my packages and letters out on time if I'm forced to stand in line here? I'm already behind as it is.

"I'm supposed to organize the mail in the evening and deliver it during the day," Posta explained. "But all my nights are full now! The zoo, the theater, the doctor, the planetarium… what a waste!"

Star, who was a few Midlandians ahead in line, turned around. "Hey!" she said. "Don't blame me. Everyone loved my solar show the first time around. And that's a fact."

"You're right," replied Posta. "I usually like going to the bakery, your shows, and everyone else's when I can. But it's crazy to be forced to go to all of them, all of the time."

"That sure as Jupiter wasn't my idea," Star retorted.

"Hey, please don't argue," said Violet.

Posta nodded. "You're right," she said. "I'm sorry for snapping, Star."

"I'm sorry, too," Star apologized.

Broadway burst out of the bakery doors. He took a

huge chomp from his muffin. "Ooh, this blueberry muffin I was forced to buy is scrumptious!" he said sarcastically.

He noticed a slip of paper in his bite of muffin. Broadway took the paper from his mouth and read it. "Be a Builda Believer!" he cried. "Yeah, right! I wasted all that money putting in new seats. But since Theater Thursday, not one Midlandian has been free for an encore!"

Broadway stalked back toward his theater. "It's a tragedy…" he muttered.

"That's Broadway for you," Zeke said with a grin.

After everyone bought and ate a muffin, it was time to meet in the Portal Theater.

Sensei was standing on the stage. Chief Tatupu was sitting in a chair to his left. There was a chair for Builda to Sensei's right, but it was empty.

The crowd assembled inside and took their seats. Zeke and Violet sat near the front row.

"We are almost ready to begin," Sensei announced. "First, each candidate will give one final speech. Chief Builda will go first, and her challenger will go second. After, we may vote. Are there any questions?"

The Midlandian audience remained quiet.

"Excellent!" said Sensei. "Then we are just waiting on the arrival of one Midlandian." He glanced toward

Builda's empty chair on the stage.

The crowd grumbled.

Zeke shifted in his seat toward Violet and Belinda. "Do you think she's even going to come to the challenge?" he asked.

"I don't know," Violet replied. "Nobody's seen her since she and Chief had that talk."

As if on cue, the stage door opened and Builda walked in. As always, it seemed, she was wearing her crown and carrying her scepter. Her new cloak was draped across her back.

"Welcome, Chief Builda," said Sensei. "Are you ready to give your final speech?"

Builda nodded.

Sensei hopped off the stage and sat in the audience.

Builda removed her cloak and hung it over her chair. She stepped to center stage and took a deep, nervous breath. She did not seem excited to speak.

"Dearest Midlandians," she began. "It has been a busy and sometimes difficult week. I made many changes in our lives. I tried to make innovations that would bring everyone happiness. However, many of my decisions have been unfair."

Many audience members murmured in agreement.

"I apologize deeply to everyone here," said Builda.

She turned to face Chief Tatupu. "You were right to challenge me," she told him. "I have made unwise choices. But I want to change that."

Builda removed the crown from her head. "That is why I have chosen to step aside as chief," she said.

Zeke, Violet, and the rest of the audience all gasped in surprise.

Builda offered the crown and scepter to Chief Tatupu. "I would like to return these to their rightful owner," she said.

The crowd clapped quietly.

Chief Tatupu stood, but he did not take the crown or scepter from Builda.

"I appreciate this gesture," said Chief, "but I cannot simply take these items back. I am not their rightful owner."

Chief's response was beginning to make Zeke nervous. "What is he talking about?" he asked Violet.

"The crown and scepter are symbols of being a leader," Chief continued. "The chief might use them, but he or she does not own them. They really should belong to all Midlandians. And that means that all Midlandians should have a say in who is their chief.

"So," he concluded, "I will only accept the crown and scepter if that is what the people of Midlandia wish."

Sensei returned to the stage. "Let us vote!" he declared. "Who wishes to see our friend Manupu, of the family Tatupu, return to the role of chief?"

Zeke and Violet looked back into the audience. Hands shot up all across the theater. Zeke could even see Vincent's bandaged thumb sticking up near the back.

Sensei scanned the crowd and counted the hands. It looked as if everyone wanted Chief Tatupu back. "I believe that Midlandia has spoken!" he said.

Everyone clapped loudly.

Builda held out the crown and scepter once more. "I would like to present you with this crown and scepter," she told Chief. "As you take them, you also take the title of chief."

Chief Tatupu knelt down in front of Builda and closed his eyes. Builda handed him the scepter. She placed the crown on his head.

"Now that's a perfect fit," Violet whispered to Belinda.

"Now," Builda intoned, "rise, Chief Tatupu!"

A roar of approval sounded throughout the theater.

"Silence," said Chief. "Silence, please!"

The audience settled down. Sensei returned to his

seat. Builda sat in her chair on the stage.

"Thank you for your support," said Chief. "As Builda said, a lot has changed this week. In my first act as your leader, I would like to eliminate all special holidays that have been introduced since the Chief for a Day contest."

The crowd burst into applause. Even the Midlandians who had been given holidays, from Broadway to Wilda to Bun, smiled and clapped.

"Cirrus, my friend," said Chief. "No longer will you be called the guesser-man. Your title is restored to weatherman. Predict away!"

Cirrus literally jumped out of his seat for joy.

"Doc Fixit," Chief called out. "You may leave the bike factory basement and return to your normal office."

Violet saw Doc Fixit and Brushy in the audience. The siblings each gave each other a high five and a hug.

"I have just eliminated many new changes and rules," Chief announced. "But there are two new rules that I would like to create. The first is about Builda."

The crowd began to boo. Builda looked down in embarrassment.

"That is not how Midlandians treat one another," said Chief. "Yes, this has been a strange week. But Builda deserves the respect you would show any other

Midlandian. She should not be treated any differently than before. I will not allow any name calling or unkindness toward her."

Zeke and Violet led a round of praise and cheers. Builda cracked a smile at Chief.

"My second announcement is about the Chief Challenge," Chief continued.

"I meant what I said before," he said. "All Midlandians own this crown and scepter. So, from now on, every four years on this day, we will have an election for chief of Midlandia. Everyone will vote and choose who will lead best. Thank you!"

Chief exited the stage door to thunderous applause. Builda left after him.

Slowly, the Midlandians left the Portal and returned to work. Zeke and Violet found Chief and Builda walking outside together. Builda had her bike and helmet at her side.

Chief removed the crown from his head. "This thing is still a bit too flashy for me," he told Builda.

"Welcome back, Chief," said Zeke.

"Hi, kids!" replied Chief.

"Belinda says congratulations," said Violet.

Builda pointed to Violet's basket. "May I pet her?"

she asked.

Violet looked at Builda doubtfully.

"Remember what I said, Violet," stated Chief.

Violet nodded and opened the basket's lid. "Just be gentle," she said.

Belinda peeked out of the basket. Builda lightly petted her fur. "I'm sorry for getting you sick," she told Belinda. "It was an accident, but that's no excuse."

"Thank you," Violet said happily. She closed the lid to protect Belinda from the sun.

"I'd better ride off," said Builda. "I have a factory to run and some sick fish to care for."

She strapped on her bike helmet. "I think this looks better on my head, don't you?" she asked. The kids nodded.

"See you around!" said Builda. She climbed on her bike and rode off.

Chief focused on Zeke and Violet. "Thank you so much for your assistance," he said. "There is just one last thing I need help with. It is very important."

"What is it?" asked Zeke.

"Cleaning up my office!" cried Chief. He headed for the community center. The kids laughed and followed him.

"I am serious, kids," said Chief. "This is no laughing matter. Builda moved everything around on me. It is a total disaster area. I do not know what she was—"

"No unkindness, Chief," Violet reminded him.

Chief smiled and quieted down. "Fair enough, Violet," he said. "Fair enough."

DISCUSSION QUESTIONS

Why did Builda want to become chief? What actions did she take to become chief?

How were Chief Tatupu and Builda different as leaders?

Why did Builda give so many Midlandians their own special day? Do you think she was trying to do a good thing?

What were some problems that came up while Builda was chief?

Why did Builda have a change of heart?